THE WRIGHT BROTHERS

A Lesson in Grit and Tenacity

THE HISTORY HOUR

"Before the Wright Brothers, no one in aviation did anything fundamentally right; since the Wright brothers, no one has done anything fundamentally different."

— DARYL COLLINS, U.S. PARK SERVICE

CONTENTS

PART I
Forward — 1

PART II
Introduction — 5

PART III
DREAMING OF THE (PROPELLER) BLADE
Developing the Wright Stuff — 13

PART IV
DEVELOPING THE BLADE
Dreams Take Flight — 23

PART V
PERFECTING THE BLADE
The World Takes Flight — 41

PART VI
PROTECTING THE BLADE
From Airmen to Attorneys — 57

PART VII
Afterword — 63

PART VIII
Further Reading — 67

Your Free eBook! — 71

❧ I ❧
FORWARD

※

Why should anyone, who is not interested in Aviation or History, be interested in the Wright Brothers? What do their life and struggle have to add to the lives of the common person out there? Do world changers possibly have more in common with us than many of us realize?

※

As you will read in this book, you'll find the many challenges encountered by the Wright Brothers in their lives. The buzzwords of the business world today all encompass what the Wright Brothers possessed in great abundance; grit, perseverance, determination, and a no quit attitude.

※

How many times have you, as a professional or in your personal life, been knocked down or told you weren't good enough? How many defeats have you suffered, leaving you to question if you should try again or just give up on the dream?

※

The dream of flight was a lifelong pursuit for the Wright Brothers. Their first experience with the pursuit of flight involved a child's toy. They loved that toy and eventually broke it. How many hours did the brothers put into fixing that toy before achieving their goal of allowing it to fly again? When it became unfixable, how many tweaks did they have to make to their own creation, a toy helicopter that they built, before a flying it?

※

How many tweaks do you need to make in your life? When do you stop? Do you stop or is life a lifelong pursuit of perfection and a series of recalibrations? That is what successful people understand and the character trait in which they possess. These men weren't necessarily smarter than you; heck they didn't go to college or have formal training in engineering, and yet, they found a way.

※

If you have a dream, as the Wright Brothers did, don't give up on it. The dream is the first step towards achieving success, and that is what the Wrights did. They dreamt it, visualized it, and spoke it; they knew they would fly someday and told others what their future successes would look like.

Learn from their story and from similar stories of successful leaders. You can achieve any goal as long as you keep working towards it, no matter how many times it takes. Success in life, or in inventing, isn't a matter of how smart you are, but about the level of your work ethic.

❧ II ☙
INTRODUCTION

☙❧

From the earliest days of human history, when the early man finally became a sentient being, they most likely looked longingly into the sky for refuge and for a competitive advantage. Early men had a difficult life semicolon, not only were they pursued by larger and more Adept predators, but they also had to hunt and gather for food to survive. Once the stressors were understood by early prehistoric man, they must have wondered to themselves,

"what if I could fly like a bird?"

How would that make life different and possibly easier?

☙❧

The human dream for flight has been around for millennia if not longer. For thousands of years within the recorded history of man, mankind saw a way to take it to the skies, not just for the thrill or for pleasure, but also for an advantage in Warfare, travel, and a better quality of life. These hopes and desires of mankind we're left as the stuff of Dreams. With the Renaissance in the Middle Ages and eventually the Industrial Revolution, mankind was finally on the precipice of taking a dream to a possible reality. Still, however, even some of the greatest Minds such as Leonardo DaVinci could not crack the elusive nature of powered flight for a man.

※

As most of us know, the dream of life did not occur until 1903 by the Wright brothers. Why do we find the Wright brothers so fascinating? What can we learn from these individuals that can be applied to our lives? Most of us will not become aerospace engineers or pilots, and happily find Wright brothers so intriguing. What questions from termites can we have that can be applied to our own? What made them different from hundreds of thousands of sciences, engineer, and dreamers before then? What further somewhere days? Why does your life matter to us today?

※

One of the main themes that are insecurely woven throughout the lives of the Wright brothers, Wilbur and Orville, is their determination. Their fighting spirit. Tenacity to never give up. They had extreme perseverance and could not be disillusioned for Long by defeats. Though they were not trained by Scholars or scientists, their work ethic and attention to details and their intentions for asking why let them to several careers in which they were successful. Each success led to another Pursuits in another success.

※

They had Supreme confidence in their abilities and in their work ethic. They truly believed that they were not smarter than anyone but that they could outwork and out hustle anyone. Idiosyncrasies and human quirks made them ideal amateur scientists. We should use the term amateur scientist with caution when speaking of the Wright brothers, because, even though they were not trained Scholars, they did employee the scientific methods in too many of their experiments and collection of data.

※

They were firm Believers in trial and error. With this philosophy and mode of research and development, the Wright brothers, like many other inventors and scientists, would dare open the doors despite hundreds upon hundreds of failures before they would achieve success. When it comes to scientific matters and Engineering exploits, often times one small variable can make the difference between a total success and a total failure. Only through this acceptance of the possibility of failure, success can be achieved eventually.

※

The Wright brothers. They did not fear defeat, but rather, use defeat as a learning opportunity, to make adjustments, to recalibrate, and to try once again. This was a process throughout their life whether it was at the printing press, their bike shop, conducting experiments at the wind tunnel, or developing and learning the principles of flight. Most of what we do today in the aviation field was first thought out by and created as best practices by the Wright brothers. They did so much more than just develop and invent a machine for flight, they developed an entire industry and profession.

☙❦❧

From a young age, they learned not to accept no as an answer. They learned to ask the question – '***why not?***' Individuals who do not accept no as a final answer are the ones who find success with in life. They are the Trailblazers and will find a way to get to their goal and destination. They do not succumb to pressure or disappointment, but they keep on pressing. Each failure makes them stronger and more determined rather than burning them up and defeating them. These are some of the greatest lessons that we, in the modern-day, can learn from these incredible entrepreneurs, inventors, and World Changers.

☙❦❧

The Wright brothers we're lucky for the family that they were born into. Their father, a man of the cloth, instilled in them many Scholastic qualities but also hammered the idea of the ability to do things. This led the Wright brothers in developing into ingenious, observant, and methodical human beings. They had amazing attention to detail and a penchant for doing research. Research is not the most glamorous or fascinating Pursuits in life and must be supplemented with an innate intellectual curiosity. This curiosity leads researchers to take the initiative and interest in problems that plagued the world and find solutions to them.

❦

Whether one is an actor, an athletes, a businessman, an aspiring politician, or an aspiring leader, the Wright brothers can provide an Outlook and philosophy of thinking for life. A philosophy of seeking out the victory from the jaws of defeat. A philosophy of never giving up and pushing on no matter what the cost. They are the individuals who laugh when people say this cannot be achieved. Keep in mind, for most of human history, even several minutes before observing the miracle of flight, human beings were skeptical of the ability to fly. Once that goal was achieved, inhuman doubt was destroyed, and the potential grew exponentially. A similar example would be the 4-minute mile. For hundreds of years, various scientists and sportsman debated and claimed that it was impossible for a human being to run a mile in under 4 minutes. With the supposed experts telling athletes that it was physically impossible, the brain could not see Victory insights. All it took was for one man to shatter that barrier, and then, more and more individuals achieved the same feat. Once they believed that they were not limited in their abilities, they were able to achieve more than the so-called experts expected. This is exactly what the Wright brothers did for mankind in their pursuit of flight.

❦

As you read these next few chapters and possibly go on to further study of the Wright brothers, it is our hope that you look into their lives and study their human determination and the characteristics that made them successful. That is the true lesson from studying their lives. Certainly, we could learn about Aviation in aerospace engineering from studying the Wright brothers, but the most important lessons that we can learn from their lives is their indomitable spirit to succeed, to soar high above the clouds, both in their thoughts and physical aspirations. Because of the Wright brothers and their machine that conquered the constraints of gravity, we as a human race are no longer limited by the sky but by the dreams that we are able to invoke within our minds.

III
DREAMING OF THE (PROPELLER) BLADE

"The desire to fly is an idea handed down to us by our ancestors who...looked enviously on the birds soaring freely through space...on the infinite highway of the air."

WILBUR WRIGHT

DEVELOPING THE WRIGHT STUFF

※

Stating the obvious that the Wright Brothers invented the first functional and controllable airplane does not do these entrepreneurial and innovative men any justice. They were accomplished businessmen, engineers, scholars, and gritty fighters to find the truth to a problem. They were masters of perseverance; a trait that they were imbued with by their Father.

※

And, they were brothers, they were partners. As a Biographer, it is difficult to lump the two into one, but it is in this inseparable, fraternal bond that made them both so great, so persistent, and so successful despite roadblocks that would emerge from time to time. While a singular individual may not have persevered and continued the fight, the brothers took turns, motivating and raising each other up to the challenges that lay before them.

❦

The sons of Bishop Milton Wright of the Church of the United Brethren of Christ and Susan Wright, Wilbur and Orville Wright were born in the years 1867 and 1871 respectively. One of the few special advantages the boys had in their lives was being born into a family where intellectual curiosity was fostered. They weren't born rich or to an aristocratic family but were born to a warm and loving family. There were 7 children in all, two of which died in their infancy. Though they were born four years apart, the brothers had a strong sense of family and loyalty to each other and to their parents. These characteristics would serve them well.

❦

Wilbur Wright was born on April 16, 1867, near an Indiana town called Millville. He was the middle child of the five living children from the family. Wilbur, as a child, has often been considered bright and very studious for his age, with an exacting and challenging mind that required much attention. Beyond his academic potential, Wilbur was a typical child who enjoyed playing and exercising gross motor skills through play. He needed a playmate, and he found one, four years later; Wilbur took very well to his younger brother Orville.

❦

Orville Wright was born four years later, on August 19, 1871. He was born into a home with no running water and no electricity. There was much that the Wright's didn't have but what they had in plentiful supply was the literary stimulation in the form of books. This library played well into the strengths of the young Orville, as he was seen as a curious young boy. This curiosity and sense of adventure also gave him a bit of a reputation for being mischievous. Later in life, Orville would state in his memoirs how lucky he and his siblings were to grow up in a home that encouraged investigation of items that piqued their interest.

※

Despite Orville's ability to study, and for being known today as a researcher and development pioneer, he didn't have much of an education. Too distracted by the world and his desires, Orville would eventually make the decision to drop out of high school during his senior year at Dayton High School to pursue his other interests.

※

The early years of Wilbur and Orville Wright saw their family travel a lot through the Midwest while their father was busy, preaching to various towns and attending to church matters. Wilbur was born in Millville, Indiana, and the family then moved one year later to Hartsville, Indiana. One year later, they would then move to Dayton, Ohio, which would eventually become their permanent home. The family took to Dayton and bought a home there and quickly had to put it up for rent, as they would then live in Cedar Rapids, Iowa, for three years only to then move to Richmond, Indiana, for three years, and they then returned home to Dayton for good in 1884. Much of this constant movement and transience caused the boys to not have the typical childhood or school career.

※

While some individuals might see this as a detriment to the development of children, this perceived weakness actually led to strength between the two boys, depending upon each other as brothers and friends, the two were oftentimes considered "***Inseparable,***" like twins. But they were not totally identical; they each had their own strengths and weaknesses. In many ways, the Wright brothers were said to have perfectly complemented each other.

When their father, Milton Wright, was appointed as Bishop in 1878, a sense of normalcy and permanence took shape as the Wright family remained residents in Dayton Ohio. While the Bishop still traveled extensively, the family was left at home to set down roots and give the family some normalcy. One of the favorite leisure activities of the family was reading the extensive Library that the family owned. While their home and furnishings were modest and very typical, the bishop and his family took great pride in their vast collection of books. This library and intellectual curiosity enabled Wilbur and Orville, in particular, to learn and do great things.

Though their father was not a college graduate, he was a man of the cloth, and therefore, had some proclivity towards the scholarship. Despite this emphasis on academic work and Divinity, the bishop instilled in his boys the notion of being able to do as well learn. It was an engineering mindset that the bishop gave his boys, and they took it to heart.

One of the most well-known stories of their childhood involves a toy that the bishop brought home to the boys one day in 1878. It was a toy helicopter of sorts, made up of paper, cork, and bamboo. In this toy, there was a rubber band that would allow the propeller to spin and cause the toy helicopter to fly upwards into the sky.

※

The boys were enamored with this incredibly miraculous toy. They played with it so much that it eventually broke. But being the industrious young men that they were, the boys reverse-engineered the toy and were able to not only repair it but build similar toys of their own making. This would eventually lead to the building of more sophisticated kites, further entrenching the young brothers into the love and dream of flight. From a young age, the boys were interested in aviation and aerospace engineering.

※

As any inventor or engineer knows, perseverance is a major strong suit for future engineers. The boys were preached to the importance of perseverance and not quitting by their father. Repairing and creating toy helicopters was only the beginning for the Wright brothers. Wherever their minds wandered off to, the boys found a way to entertain their most ambitious thoughts.

※

Considered by many historians as great inventors and scientists, it is interesting for individuals to learn that the boys were not scientists or trained engineers. Due to movement of the family and a particular accident while playing a game Loosely based on hockey, and which Wilbur suffered a major injury to his mouth and teeth that would derail his school plans, the Wright brothers did not pursue College nor did they complete High School.

※

Prior to the accident, Wilbur was intent on attending Yale and studying as a divinity student, possibly following in his Father's footsteps. But when playing a form of hockey during his senior year, a known neighborhood bully apparently threw his stick, whether intentional or not, at the face of Wilbur. This injury caused Wilbur a great deal of pain, misery, and depression, from which he could not escape for several months. This derailed the rest of his high school education and any thoughts of attending University.

※

Trying to find some purpose in their lives, Orville gave into his distracted mind, dropped his studies at the local high school and set off to create a newspaper. Not having the funds for Capital, Orville, ever the innovator, fashioned a printing press out of an old tombstone. In March of 1888, the *West Side News* published its first issue. Wilbur, needing a purpose in his life, joined his brother and helped launch the business. The brothers were successful in finding clients who bought advertisements in their papers. The paper was a minor success, affording the brothers a modest living, with which they could build upon their entrepreneurial ideas.

※

When it comes to success, a bit of luck is usually required, and at this particular time in American history, the popularity of the safety bicycle was rising. No longer the dangerous bikes with one giant wheel and one small wheel that was difficult to ride, the safety bicycle had two wheels that were of the same size. This change in the design allowed the bicycle to be a pursuit of the average American and sales were beginning to soar.

※

Already having a mechanical mind, the boys took to the bicycle and were excited by the freedom it gave people as well as by the engineering that went into creating a bike and subsequent better versions.

※

Leaving their newspaper to a family friend to run, the boys now set their sights on creating a bicycle shop. The Wright bicycle Exchange was open for business, and the boys were in the market for repairing and selling bicycles. Being one of the first bicycle shops in town, the boys did good business in the beginning. However, competition did begin to rise, and their sales fell off for a while. They started to question their business acumen and whether or not they had the aggressive nature to be a successful businessman. Just as soon as they began to doubt their abilities, they persevered and started creating and designing their own bicycles.

※

They designed a bicycle called the Van Cleve in 1896, which was guaranteed to travel further and longer than any other bicycle or tires out there. Through their engineering and approach towards efficiency, the bicycle came in at about 20 pounds. It was a sought-after bicycle for those enthusiasts who wanted the best ride. The success would fuel their desires for flights. The Wright Brothers' bike business fueled their pursuit of aviation while they were still owners through 1907.

※

One could argue that the Entrepreneurial Spirit of the Wright brothers and their entry into the small business helped pave the way for a world-changing event; the creation of the first heavier than air and steerable airplane.

❦ IV ❦
DEVELOPING THE BLADE

"If birds can glide for long periods of time, then... why can't I?"

ORVILLE WRIGHT

DREAMS TAKE FLIGHT

EMPLOYING THE WRIGHT STUFF

☙❧

Bike manufacturing was the perfect occupation for the brothers because it involved one of the exciting mechanical devices of the time, the bicycle. When the brothers took up the goal of manned flight, they already had a solid grounding in mechanics and the knowledge of how to engineer and test their ideas. Their work in bicycles was a major influence that gave them the belief and proof that an apparently unstable vehicle, such as a bike or airplane, could be balanced and steered under the control of a rider or pilot.

☙❧

With this realization and conclusion, the brothers fundamentally accepted that the manned flight was a real possibility.

With that stance, they decided to operate as scientists and researchers and read everything they could find on the subject of flight to better understand what those in previous years have attempted. They would learn from the successes and disregard the failures.

※

It is important to point out that this was not their first attempt that the Wright brothers took towards creating a powered flight. Thinking back to their childhood, the brothers often thought of that toy helicopter that their father had brought them. They had already successfully created and flew a powered vehicle in the form of that toy. If they could achieve success at a small scale, why couldn't they do so on a larger scale? This was their hope and the source of their tenacity.

※

Individuals with perseverance know that they can go back to previous successes and learn from it and build their confidence based upon it. While it was just a toy helicopter to some, it was still, nonetheless, a success. Now all the brothers had to do was use the same mechanics and concepts and apply them at a much larger scale.

※

As the brothers poured over the available literature in various local libraries, it struck both of them that they had told many in their childhood that they would achieve manned flight. When frustration and dead-ends presented themselves in the project, it was not hard to believe that the brothers thought about the time they were caught by their teacher with the toy helicopter in class, and how they confidently explain to him that they planned on building a flying machine, big enough to carry not just one of them, but both of the brothers. The teacher's scoffing at the idea further inflamed their passions and desire for success.

※

Before the brothers could have the luxury of being able to take time for research and development, they had to have enough capital and the ability to find such leisure time for better endeavors such as flight. Because of their successful businesses, in the forms of the newspaper and the bike shop, the Wright brothers were able to afford that time, devoted to researching and studying aeronautics.

※

Aviation being in its infancy, the Wright brothers had few researchers from which to learn from. Two of them stood out to the Wright brothers, Octave Chanute in the United States and Otto Lilienthal in Germany.

※

Being admirers of these two aviation pioneers, the brothers were quite devastated when they learned of Lilienthal's death in 1896 during a glider accident. Wilbur especially spent many days studying up on Lilienthal's designs, concepts, and ideas and came to the realization that successful flights were dependent upon having total control over the airframe, which was that the standard procedure for earlier attempts in flight.

※

Observing what their colleagues were creating and achieving, with Otto and his gliders and Chanute with his gliders near Lake Michigan, these breakthroughs made the brothers believers that powered flight was just within their grasp.

※

Over time, the library could only provide so much information. Once the Wright brothers had gone over all the research that they could find that was present in their general vicinity, Wilbert took it upon himself to write to the Smithsonian Institution in May of 1899. In this request, he asked for all the information in a listing of Publications about human flight. He stated that they were most interested in the problems associated with powered and mechanical human flight.

※

Within 3 weeks of sending out this letter to the Smithsonian, an official by the name of Richard Rathbun responded to Wilbur's request. In this response from the Smithsonian, the official sent a few pamphlets in a listing of books that would steer the brothers in the right direction. The official biographer of the Wright brothers went on to say that this might have been the most important Exchange in the history of the Smithsonian.

※

It is amazing to think but that Smithsonian official had set the world on a new course of human history. Because of the information that Rathbun presented to the brothers, they were well on their way to begin their research and development in the design and mechanics of the first powered airplane. From this information, they would spend the next three months, pouring over the information gained by their predecessors.

※

The fundamental change in attitude towards the problem of manned flight came in the realization that the plane had to be controllable in all three dimensions of flight, of three axes of motion; pitch, yaw, and roll. Wilbur, in particular, had observed that birds would change the angles of their wings in order to have their bodies roll left or right into a turn; a very similar body movement is used when riding a bike. One does not just turn the handlebars to turn; this would result in a crash. Rather, bike riders lean or roll into the turn, changing the angle of the wheel complemented by the slight turn in the handlebars. It is a two-step process to turn, not just one.

※

The new question or problem now was how to introduce a roll into the manmade wings or an aircraft. Again, the Wrights were in uncharted academic territory here; they had to develop and test new ideas and strategies. After spending considerable mental effort in finding a solution, the Wright brothers, ever the engineers, found their answer through a hands-on approach with the material; Wilbur discovered "***wing warping***" when he inadvertently was twisting an inner tube box. He, in essence, happened to place his thumb and forefinger on opposite corners, creating a diagonal.

※

When he squeezed his thumbs and fingers together, this would twist the box, causing the surfaces of the box to rotate in opposite directions. From this "***laboratory***" observation, Wilbur realized that the same principle could be applied to the wings of the plane. Cables could be attached to the opposite ends of the wings, and the pilot could warp the wings to help him roll into the turn, just like a bird or bike rider can.

※

With one wing turned up, and the other wing turned down, the plane would role in the direction of the turned down wing, in use of both aerodynamics and gravity. Basically, an imbalance in lift would be created, causing one end to rising and the other to fall, allowing the plane to roll. It seems like an easy concept to us today, but remember, these principles had to be discovered. The Wrights were pioneers in finding out information on their own through trial and error.

※

Utilizing the scientific method, the brothers build upon the work of others and then advanced new ideas and theories. This new idea and embracing of roll control over a plane was a groundbreaking and revolutionary idea. This revolutionary idea would eventually lead to the first successful flight, but countless numbers of test sessions had to be made first.

※

The brothers first tested the novel concept via kites that were designed with strings attached in the diagonal design to allow Wilbur to bend the wings of the kite. They did this kite testing in Dayton near their home. Once they realized that this system was working, they then set their sights on creating a full-sized glider.

⁂

In the creating and testing of a full-sized glider, the brothers were researching locations that would have consistent high winds and preferably and landing zone that was a bit softer than to deal with the inevitable crashes and failures they would encounter. Being the scientifically minded men that they were, again, with no formal training, they reached out to the US Weather bureau for direction in where they could find a suitable location for their testing.

⁂

Through their research from the weather bureau, the brothers happened upon to Kitty Hawk in North Carolina. Not only it was a suitable location, but it wasn't that far from Dayton Ohio. What the brothers learned was that it was one of the consistently windiest places in the nation. It was very similar to the sand dunes of Lake Michigan that their predecessors had used. It didn't have many trees, it had sand hills that were high enough for launching their experimental aircraft, and of course, the beaches made of sand provided a soft cushion for crashes when they would occur.

⁂

Finally, from an innovation standpoint, it was a pretty isolated area that allowed the brothers to design and test their aircraft without many prying eyes. While those observers who may have seen the experiments may have laughed, other enterprising individuals might see it as an opportunity to steal all of the research and development they had poured many years into acquiring.

❧

And their correspondence with Joseph Dasher, the head of the weather bureau, the brothers also had enough luck to get an invitation from the postmaster William Tate in his family with a promise of helping them in their efforts in Kitty Hawk North Carolina. With a suitable location now determined, the brothers went to work on building and assembling their full-sized glider.

❧

They begin work on a full-sized glider in Ohio at the end of 1899 and in the spring of 1900. Disney glider included the new development of wing warping for the purposes of rolling into turns. Their new revolutionary idea that they were betting would help them succeed. When the glider was ready, and the weather conditions were proper, the brothers disassembled the glider and took it down to Kitty Hawk. Upon their arrival, they reassembled it and first flew it as a kite. If this kite experiment worked, they would then fly themselves, with a Target date of September 1900.

❧

With William Tate's home as a headquarters for the experiments, the Wright brothers used a sewing machine on their property to stitch together the fabric that would compose the lighters wings. This partnership with the tape family was invaluable to the first steps of Aviation as well.

Once the wings were affixed to the glider, the brothers set out in October of 1900 with their glider, retrofitted as a kite for now and went to Kill Devil Hills, which was about four miles south of Kitty Hawk North Carolina. With their full-sized kite, the brothers went into experimentation mode and flew their kite, thanks to ropes and lines that were connected to the bottom of the plane, much like a kite hanging down to the ground where the brothers would steer the plane.

While seeing a scene of momentous on successful kite flying, he's given the brothers a sense that their flying apparatus would work. With approaching winter, the brothers disassembled their kite and packed up for home. For the next three years, the brothers would enter into a period of time where they would create gliders, conduct experiments, disassemble, and move on to a bigger glider. With each success, however, many failures came into play, and at times, the brothers would become despondent and frustrated with their work. Their perseverance and teamwork as brothers helped them fight through the tough times that could have derailed the experiments and research.

As researchers who were heavily invested in the work of their predecessors, the Wright brothers were particularly appreciative of a visit in August of 1901 by Octave Chanute to observe their experiments and test flights in Kitty Hawk. Like the Wright brothers, Chanute was one of the leading authorities in aviation and, in particular, gliders. Being the perfectionists that the Wright brothers were, and with one of their idols observing, they were disappointed with how their new glider handled, however, their colleague Chanute was completely amazed and excited for what the future of Aviation held based on their new glider. Despite the good comments from Chanute, the brothers headed home, once again with the feeling as if their progress was not good enough.

❦

It almost felt like divine intervention, but over the winter months when the Wright brothers were feeling down about their progress, their College Chanute invited Wilburn to make a presentation to the Western Society of Engineers. This adulation from a respected colleague reinvigorated Wilbur and his brother to continue on with the experiments and research. Through the writing of this article, Wilbur found that the scientific data and work of predecessors that had been accepted as valid was now being called into question. Wilbur being the inquisitive man that he was, set out to test the accuracy of these lift tables and other data. In another major milestone for aviation, Wilbur created a small wind tunnel, from which he could test out various wing designs and scientific data. With this wind tunnel, Wilbur was able to test for lift and drag in different Wing foil designs. In all, Wilbur would test more than 200 wings from these experiments; he went on to investigate the top 50 of them that seems promising for the full-sized airplane.

❦

With new scientific research and data, the Wright brothers eventually started making Wing designs made of sheet metal. The use of the new material was another major step in the

right direction for the Wright brothers. While
making amazing scientific discoveries, this new body
was very demanding of both our time and scholarly
They certainly could have made great strides if they ha
assistance to help them. Once again, it is important to point
out that the Wright brothers had no formal scientific training, and yet, they changed the course of history. It took
tenacity and grit for the brothers to keep working day after
day and failure after failure. Where most men would fail, the
Wright brothers persevered.

Over the course of the next year-and-a-half, the Wright
brothers once again came to Kitty Hawk with a larger and
improved glider. With the data and information gained from
the wind tunnel, their third glider presented enormous
improvements and research developments over their previous
gliders. This new glider allowed for greater lift, which meant
longer flights. Through trial and error and the realization that
the glider kept diving downward, the Wright brothers turn to
another obstacle into a strength when they change the fixed
tail to a movable rudder, and they instinctively linked the
rudder to the wing warping controls so that the pilot would
roll through a hip cradle, and the rudder wood pivot in the
right direction, which would allow the glider to move in a
similar fashion to a bicycle where a rider would use their hips
to roll into a turn.

With this new glider and their new designs, the Wright
brothers made over 1000 glides, some of which flew for over
600 feet. With a successful autumn, the Weight Brothers left

f 1902 with much success with their They would head home once again to e upcoming year. Upon heading home rothers felt in a better position for had previously felt in the prior year.

With enough data and experience with their gliders, the Wright brothers were convinced that they were ready to start testing engine designs for the first powered flight. Realizing that they cannot do everything on their own, they sent out letters to the most experienced internal combustion engine manufacturers from around the world. They asked for information about the possibility of creating an engine that could at least produce 8 horsepower, and it had weight restrictions of weighing no more than 180 pounds. In a surprise, the brothers were shocked to find out that no such engine could be found that met their horsepower and weight restriction guidelines. The biggest problem was that the engines were too heavy with added power, or they were too weak when built for lightness. As a mature and now Professional Engineers, they realize that they were going to need to create a lighter and more efficient engine, one that had not been created or attempted before.

The brothers reached out to Charlie Taylor, a man who had amazing engineering skills, and they gave him the plans for their plane. Charlie along with the Wright brothers had to create an innovative and new form of engine. Most revolutionary in the creation of this engine was that the engine block would be made from aluminium, which was extremely rare for the time. Aluminium is fairly strong and much lighter than steel and other metals that were traditionally used. With the engine problem being attended to by experts, the brothers next set their eyes on the problem of creating a propeller to power the plane. Once again, the brothers found themselves in a scholarly vacuum where there was no information or data available. They would once again be pioneering an entirely new scientific endeavor.

Once again, the Wright brothers showed that no matter what the problem, the severity of it or the lack of information out there, they would not be deterred from their objectives and goals. When roadblocks presented themselves, they decided to tackle the problem head-on and find solutions on their own if needed. This is one of the major characteristics of successful inventors and leaders. They do not take no for an answer; they find ways of achieving their mission and objective. It is these characteristics and ideas that allow the Wright brothers to stand out among other leaders. Even if an individual is not interested in aviation or powered flight, the Wright brothers as human beings with grit and determination should motivate and instill confidence in any reader.

The Wright Brothers finished the new aircraft over the summer of 1903, and then in late September, they left Dayton, Ohio for their camp at Kill Devil Hills. They arrived on September 25th and immediately got to work. The brothers, no strangers to adversity, kept running into delays due to a broken propeller shaft. These broken shafts led to the brothers having to return to Dayton twice to replace them.

After months of engine shaft failures and other distractions, Wilbur won a coin toss and made the first flight attempt on December 14th; the plane stalled after take-off. Though so hopeful, only after three seconds, the engine stalled, causing minor damage to the aircraft when it crashed down, setting the brothers back a few days once again. They flew for three short seconds, and some want to claim it as the first flight, but the brothers did not consider it successful. Their next attempt came on December 17th; winter was setting in, and the day was bitterly cold. A 33-degree ambient temperature with a 27-mph sustained wind, gusting across the hills, made the wind chill more around 6 degrees Fahrenheit.

※

The Wrights, so close to achieving the goal, were running out of time. They were still attempting something that never succeeded before. They were inventing the science and art of piloting a heavier than air aircraft, and they were now attempting all of this in less than ideal conditions. Orville, later on, recounting the momentous day, stated that

> *"our audacity in attempting flights in a new and untried machine, under such circumstances."*

They were stubborn and unrelenting, so they pressed on. Nothing would stop them from achieving the first flight. Not now, that they were so close to making it a reality.

※

The Wright Brothers and five men from the Kill Devil Hill's life-saving station hauled the flyer to the launching rail track once again. The brothers picked John Daniels to work the camera that day. It should be noted that John Daniels was doing something new as well; he had never used a camera before, and now here he was, tasked with taking one of the most famous pictures in history. Orville, knowing the historic event that was to occur, put Daniels and the camera about 30 feet aways from the end of the starting rail and instructed him to snap the picture, which involved squeezing a rubber bulb, to trip the shutter as the flyer passed the front of the rail.

After final checks and instructions, Orville very carefully got into the flying machine and lay down in the hip cradle. With his left hand, he held the vertical level lever that controlled the front elevator, and with his right hand, he started the engine by moving a small horizontal lever on the wing to open a fuel chute behind him. Wilbur rotated one of the propellers, and the engine fired up at 10:35 am local time.

Orville moved the starting lever, and the flyer began to move down the launching track slowly. Wilbur ran alongside the right wing, keeping it steady as best as he could, and finally, at the end of the rail, and after so many experiments and trials, and frustrations, the flier lifted into the air, and John Daniels snapped the picture for all of history to behold.

Their first flight traveled 120 feet and lasted only 12 seconds, but it was the first in the history of the world, in which a heavier than air, engine powered, and controllable plane raised itself by its own power into the air. The flight was powered forward without a decrease in velocity and flew to a point as high as the launching point.

※

For more empirical evidence, the Wrights attempted three more flights with Orville and Wilbur taking turns as the pilot covering 175 feet on flight one, 200 feet on flight two, and at noon, flown by Wilbur, covering 852 feet in 59 seconds on the last flight of the day. More flights would surely have been attempted but in the last flight, broke the front elevators of the flyer. With the damaged plane, the men then hauled the flyer back to their camp from when suddenly a powerful gust of wind flipped it over several times. Despite their attempts to hold the plane down, the plane was severely damaged and would never taste the air in flight again. The brothers shipped what was left of the plan home and put it in storage.

※

That first plane to achieve flight was put into storage in Dayton until it was restored in 1916. It was lent to several locations for display, and then in 1928, the airplane was placed on loan to the Science Museum in London England for 20 years. In 1948, the airplane was returned to the United States and permanently installed in the Smithsonian Institution Museum in Washington DC where it resides today.

V
PERFECTING THE BLADE

"The course of the flight up and down was exceedingly erratic, partly due to the irregularity of the air, and partly to lack of experience in handling this machine. The control of the front rudder was difficult on account of its being balanced too near the center."

ORVILLE WRIGHT

THE WORLD TAKES FLIGHT

A WORLD DEBUT, FINALLY

※

While the first flights in human history took place in 1903, the Wright brothers had yet to make their world debut in a sense. Making flights out of Kitty Hawk North Carolina, observers and journalists were practically nonexistent for the first flights. There were no pictures, just the one on news coverage. There were some blurbs in the local Dayton newspaper, however, reporting an event wasn't the same as it is witnessed by a multitude of people as well as being accompanied by photographs now by a videographer.

※

By 1906, the Wright brothers were in talks with France on making arrangements to sell their newest model of their plane. Still, however, neither the French nor anyone in Europe had seen the miracle of flight yet. Without visual proof, many people were in disbelief that such a feat of engineering could occur.

༺❀༻

The French newspaper the Paris Herald even had a mocking editorial that was titled flyers or Liars, calling into question the validity and accuracy of supposed stories of the brothers successfully flying in their machine.

> *"The Wrights have flown, or they have not flown, if they possess a machine, or they do not possess one, they are in fact either flyers or Liars, it is difficult to fly ellipses, it is easy to say we have flown."*

༺❀༻

In March of 1906, the Wright brothers underwent a few weeks of meetings with a French delegation, talking about their flying machine. Whether it be a marketing Ploy by the entrepreneurial Brothers to cause greater speculation and excitement around their invention, the brothers refuse to show their new flyer 3, but they were willing to show photographs of the plane and presents eyewitness testimony about the flights of the plane. One of the delegations, Commandant Bonel, the 1 of the skeptics of the group was officially convinced by the brothers that they could actually in fact fly and was impressed with the amount of research in progress they were still making for the future. With this impression finally made on the downs, he went back to friends with the possibility of the agreement still being solidified. There were still too much doubting the delegation had, however, to produce in agreement in Dayton after 2 weeks.

⚜

Even though the brothers were disappointed with the results of these meetings, they kept a good professional relationship with the commandant and wrote to him the following,

> *"Notwithstanding the failure to reach an agreement at our final conference last evening, we should always remain very friendly to you personally into your country... Allow us to express our Hardy appreciation of your uniform fairness and courtesy throughout this long conference."*

⚜

Despite the concessions beach of sorts to the friends, the scientific road was beginning to understand and believe the claims of the right brothers and the testimonies of the eyewitnesses. In the magazine, Scientific American, an article titled "***The Wright Aero Plane and its Performances***" was published. In the article, 11 eyewitnesses to the various flights answered specific questions about the machine and how it handled in the air. With such strikingly similar answers and statements by the eyewitnesses, it was now generally being accepted that the Wright brothers had in fact achieved flights.

⚜

With disbelief set in around the world, the Wright brothers

took it upon themselves to set up a tour of sorts, which included stops in Europe.

❧

The brothers knew, if they were going to make a successful World debut, they were going to have to practice the art of flying once again. Surprisingly, though addicted to the freedom and wonder of flight, neither of the brothers had flown since 1905. It had now been two and a half years since either of them had flown, and they were planning on making a public demonstration to Major crowds for the purposes of selling their machine in Europe.

❧

To get ready for their European tour, the Wright brothers once again headed off to Kitty Hawk North Carolina where they were demoralized to find that their former headquarter was in shambles, it was a complete mess. It was not good; it was not a good omen for the future seeing that the birthplace of flights was in such disarray. The brothers, the orderly people that they were, respectful of cleanliness and Order, got back to work in redeveloping the Kitty Hawk practice area. Finally, with the amenities were to their liking, the brothers began flying once again, taking baby steps and flights, lasting longer and going farther. As the practice sessions increased, reporters started arriving; the reporters started hanging around the Hills with binoculars to watch and observe the brothers in flight and in action. Even the Paris Herald, who had mocked the brothers just a year before, sent a correspondent to observe.

❧

Having a Paparazzi of swords, the brothers would have to learn to deal with the onrush of observers and journalists from now on. It was a double-edged sword. They wanted the notoriety and acknowledgements of their successes, but at the same time, the brothers were not prepared to lose out on the Privacy that they had once enjoyed. Their future flights would never be the same.

With enough practice sessions under their belts, the Wright brothers begin their Voyage to Paris France. They reached Paris on May 29th of 1908, and they started investigating possible sites for their demonstrations. When the brothers were in the French Countryside, the French journalist started proclaiming the superiority of French Pilots versus that of the Wright brothers. It became a nationalistic story, one of the French versus The Americans.

To quell some of this nationalist bravado, the Wright brothers, after seeing enough demonstration sites, eventually stated to the journalist that their secret trials were over and that the French populist would be the first to see with their own eyes that man had truly achieved flight.

Even on the official day of triumph on August eighth, 1908, the French, in skeptics, continued talking up until the successful flight. Many of the ever-growing crowd we're hoping to see a successful flight, but others were there for more devious reasons, hoping for the Americans to pull their faces and improve the flight hinder right when the flyer was not successful.

※

Much like a Vaudeville Inn production, the Wright brothers had a sense of Showmanship to them. French Observers we're feeling the countryside to be witnesses to the possibility of history-making events. They spent many hours in the hot summer sun, waiting for this momentous event that can get started. It built in them a sense of excitement and a little bit of frustration. They had all this pent-up energy in wanting to see something truly miraculous.

※

The building of tension, excitement, and a little bit of frustration continued. Even when it seemed like the flight was finally going to begin when they fired up the engine, the sound of it left them feeling uneasy, and they turn the engine off to have another look at it. The large and hot crowd was now getting antsy. A failure could possibly have been met with a riotous group of people, having spent most of their day in the hot sun, waiting to see something that many were characterizing as a bluff or a ruse.

※

Finally, after a long and hot day, full of aggravation and time-wasting buy account for the people, Wilbur was finally satisfied with the pre-flight preparations and stated to regroup gentleman,

"I'm going to fly."

❦

He got into the aircraft, and two men grabbed the propellers, pulling them downwards to start the engine. But he decided to have another check-up after hearing the engine sound, and Wilbur left the pilot seat for another inspection of the plan once again. He wanted to make sure for himself that corrections were made and that he was truly ready to fly.

❦

He finally got back into his seat, and he released the trigger, which allowed the weight on the catapult to drop. As the rail went down, Wilbur and his plane went up. The crowd burst into cheers as he flew over the trees, and then in the distance, the crowd saw the left-wing drop out of the sky. Many of them were with their mouths agape at the certainty of death that this American pilot was going to endure. Instead, they saw the left wing to drop in the plane into a roll, turning, and circling back around the crowd. He kept banking to the left and made a perfect curve flying back towards the grandstand, from which he had left. He flew at just about 30 to 35 feet over the ground and made a perfect landing about 50 feet from where he had started off.

❦

In all, this momentous flight lasted less than 2 minutes, but he had flown about 2 miles. With the long day that the French people endured, one might expect that they would have been happy just to see 10 seconds of flight. But instead, they saw almost 2 minutes, and they were all awestruck. Even those last-minute detractors and Skeptics chimed in stating that the Wright brothers can fly and that they were not bluffing. Even the French Pilots admitted that they were in their infancy compared to the Wright brothers. It was a marvelous day for France, for the aviation world, and for world history itself. Those in military uniform that was present that day left knowing that the rules of War had changed. Military men would now have to take and defend the skies. But how soon before that sort of warfare was possible?

※

The world had certainly entered into a new age. The age of flight that would change business, Commerce, Warfare and make the world a smaller place. Eventually, this power of flight would lead a man to break the bonds of gravity and escaping our atmosphere into space. The Wright brothers surely had changed the world. Not bad for a couple of high school dropouts and bike salesmen.

※

France was certainly a doubled-edged sword when the Wrights and historians look back on the momentous, exciting and world-changing event. For a brief moment, the French, and all of Europe, for that matter, were in awe of the Americans and of the Wright Brothers. As a French pilot said, after seeing their successful flight in full display in-front of thousands of his countrymen,

"We are infants compared to the Americans."

The French were just learning to crawl whereas the Wright Brothers and the Americans were taking a brisk walk in comfortable circles around their competition.

※

Like most innovations in the technology field, competitive advantage did not last for very long. Hearing the warning sounds of the drums of war, The French and the rest of Europe took to the plane, and the possibilities are afforded to the nations as the rumours of war kept getting louder. Europe knew that a deadly and costly war was coming, and perhaps it would be aviation that would hasten the end of the war in victory for the nation that had created, through research and development, the most technologically superior air force and aviators.

※

Within a year of being in awe of the Americans and of the Wright Brothers, the French were leading the charge in terms of research and development. While the Wright Brothers were content in building off the success of their Wright flyer, which was a kite design, with the elevators in the front of the plane, the Europeans were creating different looking planes and totally reimagining the airplane that the Wright Brothers gave to the world.

※

While the fuselage was practically nonexistent in the Wright flyer, the Europeans embraced the important usage of the fuselage, elongated it, allowing for longer planes, capable of carrying larger payloads. The payloads would eventually include another copilot, to fly with the pilot, sitting one behind the other, whereas, in the Wright Brothers' design, extra passengers would be side by side in the flyer.

※

Also, another major change in the design of the European airplane was the construction of the elevators in the rear of the plane. This aided the pilot from a visual standpoint, creating a more unobstructed view for the pilot and copilot to see what was in front of them. This would be particularly important in terms of air power usages a few years later in the war.

※

While the French were accepting of the power of aviation, the US Army was dragging its feet in terms of acceptance of the miracle of flight and its application to the war machine. The French were testing and experimenting with new ideas, while the Army was still requiring more proof and evidence from the Wright Brothers and whether their flyer could actually fly.

※

As the US dragged its feet, the French were destroying flight records daily, often multiple times in a single day. Within a year of accepting the challenge of flight, the French leapfrogged the Americans in terms of flight ability. They were flying higher, longer, and farther than anyone could have imagined just months before. While the Wright Brothers were fighting hard to protect their patents and their already outdated designs, the French were testing the limits of flight each and every day.

※

In steps of flights, Louis Bleriot, a French master aviator, had put in almost just as much work as the Wright Brothers had as early aviators. He had his own thoughts on plane design as well and put them to work using his own hands. Much like the Wright Brothers, Bleriot was not only the engineer of his work but also the pilot as well. It is hard to determine which of his skills was greater - that of engineer and visionary or that of a pilot in the early days of aviation.

Both skill sets were important for achieving flight and maintaining it in as safe of a manner as possible. The engineer in the Bleriot, as well as in the Wright Brothers, gave them confidence as early pilots. Considering that flight was a new human endeavor, it would be difficult for the mind to believe that dreams could be a reality without having an instrumental role in the creation and the design of the flying machine. Only by being the creator and designer, could these early pilots be so successful? They had confidence in flight because they were the ones that turned the wrenches and the screws.

Much like today, with prizes being offered for the first civilian space successes, there were prizes being offered by various groups for aviation achievements. One of the more attractive prizes was from the *Daily Mail*, offering One Thousand Pounds to the aviator who could successfully fly across the English Channel. Having proven to himself and his countrymen that he could easily span the length of the Channel, he had flown distances of twenty-five and thirty-one miles on various occasions, he set out on the mission of flying across the channel.

※

It took him about forty minutes to achieve, flying around 45-50 miles per hour, Louis Bleriot had crossed the channel from the Strait of Dover near Calais to Northfall Manor in Dover. Because of this successful crossing, he won the 1,000 pound prize and made the Europeans quickly forget the Wright Brothers.

※

When word of the momentous and important achievement reached America and the Wright Brothers, it did little to ignite a sense of urgency or the need to innovate in them. They were already in the throes of protecting the work they had already created that was already becoming an obsolete technology in the light of newer designs and models.

※

Though Europe now had their own flying heroes to follow and support in hopes of going ever higher, faster, and farther, the Wright Brothers had proven their abilities to their own country's military and were taking orders for delivery to the U.S. Army. While there were many in the Department of Defense that thought the airplane would prove to be insignificant, much like the once heralded hot air balloon, the military knew that they should at least try to keep pace with their European counterparts and prevent being totally absent as at least an exploratory flight group.

※

For the Wright Brothers, however, their aviation days as

innovators were coming to an end. Shortly after the death of a Wright in 1912, The Wright Company delivered its final plane to the U.S. Army in 1914, only to see it was dropped from the military inventory one month later. The Europeans had caught up and surpassed the Wrights, but they couldn't take away that first flight.

VI
PROTECTING THE BLADE

"The airplane stays up because it doesn't have the time to fall."

— ORVILLE WRIGHT

FROM AIRMEN TO ATTORNEYS

PROTECTING THEIR LEGACY

❦

Much like the Research and Development fields of today, innovators such as the Wright Brothers endured their share of litigation, patent infringements, plagiarism, slander, and defamation. The brothers were not so much the litigious types for financial reasons but rather, to protect their reputation and garner the acclaim, acknowledgement, and respect that they felt they deserved. Not only what they, as scientists and aerospace engineers, deserved, but what the blossoming industry of aviation deserved.

❦

While in the early days of flight, many people saw the concept of flight as a vaudevillian type of attraction or novelty, the Wright Brothers knew it was much more than a novelty, but that flight would eventually change the way the world operates and interacts. It is interesting to think that the flight was taken so un-seriously in those first two or three decades after Kitty Hawk.

※

Still, there were plenty of unscrupulous businessmen that wanted to cash in on the work that the Wright's had done with flight. After Le Mans, Wilbur Wright would only fly one more time in 1911, training a German pilot. While he and his brother wanted to fly and develop more, the brothers found themselves in legal battle after battle. This biggest curse against the Wright Company was patent infringements. Everyone wanted a piece of the flying game and was stealing the work of Wilbur and Orville who had put so many years into the development, if not a lifetime. They could not allow it. Sadly, while carrying out these courtroom battles over current innovations, other aviation researchers were making those patents irrelevant in terms of technology. The Wright Brothers innovation was being left in the dust while they fought so many legal battles.

※

With the spirit and fun of flight pulled from their lives, Wilbur embodied the aviation lives of the Wright's. Just as soon as they tasted ultimate victory in 1908 in Le Mans, their career was fading and dying. The Wright innovation was dying along with Wilbur Orville. In the spring of 1912, Wilbur was afflicted with high fevers for days upon days. He was stricken with Typhoid Fever, and his life and spirit were dwindling with each passing day. At the young age of 45 years young, Wilbur succumbed to his affliction and died on May 30, 1912. Such a young age at which to pass, but he had accomplished so much and changed the world in that time span.

※

His brother, Orville, was left alone of his greatest partner and companion - his brother. He and his sister Katherine suffered greatly over the loss. Orville also suffered in the thought that their life's work was only enjoyed for a short time by his brother. In a way, this realization caused Orville to double down in the legal efforts to protect their good names and work. It caused the Wright Company to go in the opposite direction of innovation.

※

With the ensuing death of his father, Bishop Milton Wright, in 1917, Orville was left only with his sister Katharine. The brothers loved her dearly, and she continued her support for Orville, even accompanying him for another European tour of various capital cities. By this point in their lives, they had spent a lifetime together as a family, but when they needed each other the most, they grew apart.

※

Orville was a peculiar man, just like his brother. Though he was friends with Katharine's eventual fiancé, Orville was so mad and displeased by the news that he cut off all ties and communication with his sister. This hurt her very badly and she and her new husband, Henry Haskell, moved to Kansas City. Orville refused to go to her wedding, and when she was eventually stricken with pneumonia in 1929, Orville was still refusing to see her. Finally, as she neared death, Orville made the right decision and went to see her prior to her passing. He brought her body home to Dayton and had her buried in the family cemetery.

***

Orville was now all alone in life. He had no more family, only more legal battles to fight. He was done with flying as a pilot for over ten years now. That thrill in his life was gone, just as many young pilots today are grounded for age, health, or desk duty if serving in the military. For many flyers, it seems, as soon as they start flying, they are held down on earth, always looking longingly into the sky.

***

Amazingly, the very institute that helped the Wrights to achieve flight, The Smithsonian Institute, was the same organization that caused Orville much consternation later on his life. The very man that the Wrights had offered their original 1903 Flyer to, Charles Walcott was seemingly trying to call into question whether the Wrights developed the first machine capable of flight. He even had the Langley aircraft restored and slightly improved to be relaunched to prove the machine would work and that it was a launch malfunction that prevented Langley from achieving the first flight. Because of this test of the rehabbed Langley flyer, the Smithsonian actually released a statement, stating that the Langley produced the first machine capable of flight. This was a major blow against Orville and his recently deceased brother. It called into question their life's work.

❦

To further complicate the ethics of Walcott, he then demanded that the Langley plane be restored to its 1903 condition, basically duping the public into believing that the model was capable of flight. It seemed malicious in its attempts to discredit the Wrights. Because of these dealing by the Smithsonian, Orville would eventually offer it to the Museum in London, who took care of the flyer for 20 years, before it made its way to its final destination, The Smithsonian, where one can still see it today.

❦

Orville lived a fairly comfortable life, as he would call it. He was well off, but not wealthy by his estimation. Much like many innovators of today, though he led the charge of innovation, he did not reap the rewards of his invention as he should have. Considering the effects the flight has had on the planet, The Wrights should have been obscenely wealthy, but they didn't do it for the money, but for the pursuit of finding a solution to a problem.

❦

Orville lived out the last 20 years of life, attending various memorial dedications and observing near mile markers in terms of aviation and space exploration. His Wright Flyer could barely fly 12 seconds on that first fateful flight, and in his lifetime, Orville saw war aircraft changing the way we did battle, saw the first jets, was around to see the breaking of the sound barrier, and the launching of rockets; all events that would not have occurred without the work of the Wright Brothers.

❧ VII ❦
AFTERWORD

❦❧

18 years later after the first flight, and 13 years after the triumph at Le Mans, an Army Air Corps Colonel, William "***Billy***" Mitchell, would put his military career on the line in demanding that the U.S. Military take the concept of air power more seriously. The eventual General Mitchell would go on to be court marshaled over his beliefs in the power of air warfare, but would eventually go on to be known as the father of the U.S. Air Force.

❦❧

Visionaries such as the Wright Brothers created other visionaries that could see the value and advantage of aviation and improved aircraft. Today, it almost seems like the de facto images we that have of the military warfare, and it is that of the aircrafts, bombing targets, and fighters protecting airspace. Aircraft not only changed the way the wars were fought but they also now have the capabilities of preventing war in the first place. Today, military pilots are capable of flying halfway around the world, hitting a target that may become too aggressive, stop the threat, and be home to dinner with their families. What once would take months for the end of the constant voyage by sea can now be endured in less than 24 hours of travel by air.

This advantage was not only seen by the military minded, however, but also for civilians, allowing for a new standard in terms of social mobility, and immigration from various parts of the world to other parts. Today, the world has become a global village, much smaller due to advancements in the people moving aircraft that is affordable to the mankind. Families, though separated by thousands of miles, can take solace in the fact that only a several hour flight by plane is all that separates them from their loved ones. It is quite a liberating thought for so many in the world. Considering what we know of the benefits of flights now, it is so perplexing to think that flight was almost laughable in its early days.

Despite what the early naysayers thought of human flight, the Wright Brothers were proud of their accomplishments and wanted to protect their names and reputation. They also wanted to protect the intellectual property that they created in terms of their innovative flight technologies. The Wright Brothers even found themselves in legal battles in attempts to disprove or call into question their claims to be the first to fly.

⁂

These legal headaches and battles did a lot of damage to the brothers, both physically and mentally. It also limited their amount of time to fly and to conduct further research to perfect their planes better. At the end of 1903, the man was lucky to get three seconds off the ground. By 1914, without much assists from the brothers, European aircraft were being used in wartime missions, first as reconnaissance, then bombing and fighter aircraft. Within a decade, human took the miracle of flight and weaponized it, much like any other technology is often used. It is through the military industrial complex that new technologies make leaps in terms of innovation and improvements.

⁂

Even though the Wright Brothers were dreamers and visionaries, one has to wonder if they could have possibly conceived the idea that man would go from primitive powered flight to the jet age within fifty years. Reaching Mach 10 and that manned ships would eventually go into space and to the moon. The technology and ability of flight grew exponentially during the first 75 years of the 20th Century. Sadly, from a pilot's perspective, that progression slowed down, planes aren't produced for extreme speed as they once were but now are sought after for their stealth abilities. Aviation isn't pushing the envelope anymore in terms of human flight; those requirements are now a moot point with the introduction and escalation of unmanned aircraft.

Unmanned aircraft can pull many more g's and don't have human constraints that limit their time in the air or the scope of their mission. It might make the Wright Brothers sad to think that as the technology increases, the controls are getting farther from what human beings seem to get. Eventually, the dangerous job of being a pilot, test pilot, and astronaut may be left totally to a computer with artificial intelligence. Those engineers creating these new types of aircraft are progressing towards the field of aviation, but the thrill and danger of flying off into the wild blue yonder are fading.

❧ VIII ❧
FURTHER READING

☙✦❧

If you would like to continue your studies of the Wright Brothers, there is a plethora of great books out there for kids and for adults.

☙✦❧

For detailed accounts of their lives and their trials and tribulations, both as inventors and as human beings, you should start with these three recommended books.

☙✦❧

"***The Wright Brothers***" by David McCullough and "***To Conquer the Air: The Wright Brothers and the Great Race for Flight***" by James Tobin. "***Air Power***" by Stephen

Budiansky, while not entirely about The Wrights, has a great section on their struggle to get people interested in flight. Even after the plane finally achieved flight, the war was on to get people interested in the transformative power of Air Power.

Copyright © 2018 by Kolme Korkeudet Oy

All rights reserved.

No part of this book may be reproduced in any form or by any electronic or mechanical means, including information storage and retrieval systems, without written permission from the author, except for the use of brief quotations in a book review.

YOUR FREE EBOOK!

As a way of saying thank you for reading our book, we're offering you a free copy of the below eBook.

Happy Reading!

GO WWW.THEHISTORYHOUR.COM/CLEO/

Made in the USA
Columbia, SC
24 March 2020